The abilities in me

This book is dedicated to Alfie Jones.

First edition February 2020

Published by The Abilities In Me
Written by Gemma Keir
Illustrations copyright © 2020 by Adam Walker-Parker
Edited by Claire Bunyan

ISBN Paperback:9781784566975
ISBN Hardback: 9781784566982
First printed in the United Kingdom, 2020

www.theabilitiesinme.com

The abilities in me

Hydrocephalus

Written by Gemma Keir
Illustrated by Adam Walker-Parker

I have something to share with you.
I have a condition, it's hard to see.
I have Hydrocephalus;
let me tell you more about me.

There is fluid that builds up in my brain,
it can cause pressure in my head.
It is meant to drain back into my body,
but it stays up there instead.

It can make me feel dizzy.
I get headaches and tiredness too.
I might have trouble thinking
and trying to understand you.

When I am at the hospital,
I visit a room with a big machine.
It is just like a really big camera,
that can see inside of me.

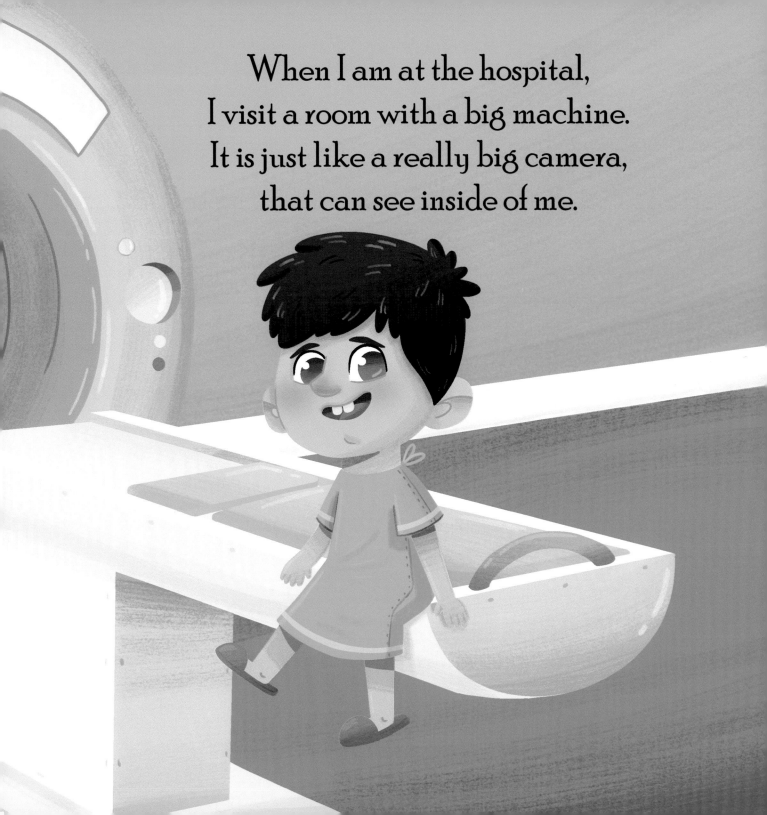

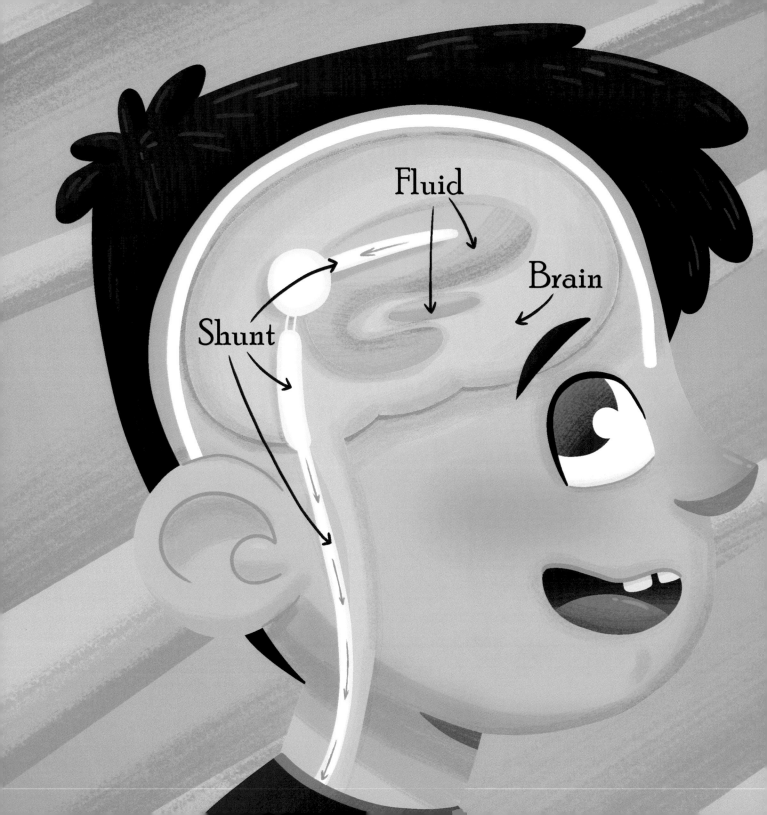

Something that you cannot see,
is a shunt inside my brain.
This is to stop the pressure,
it will help the fluid drain.

There are other children with Hydrocephalus,
but we are not all the same.
It can affect us all in many ways,
just like we have different names.

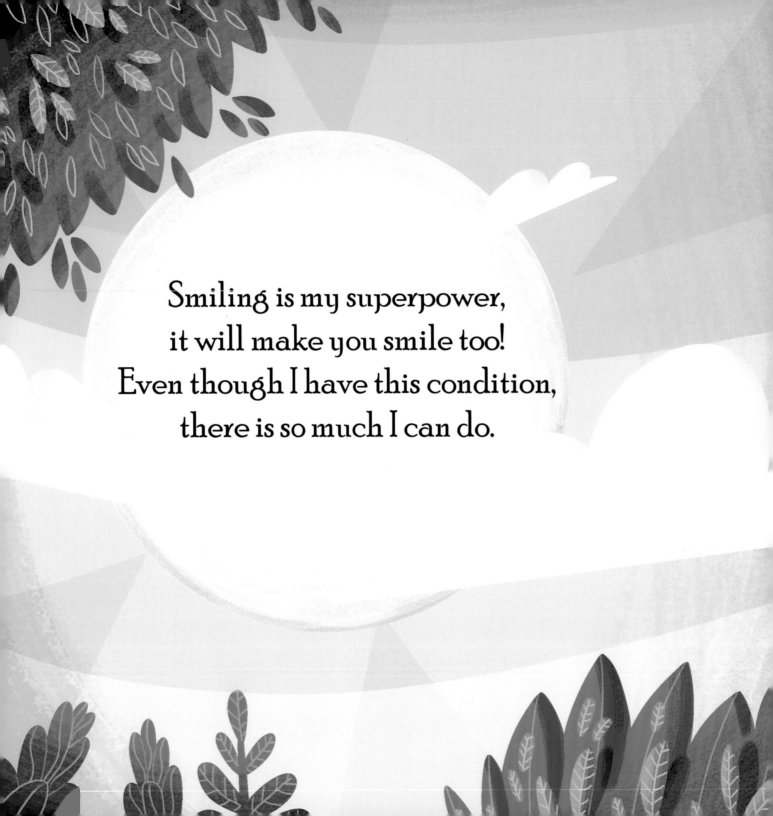

Smiling is my superpower,
it will make you smile too!
Even though I have this condition,
there is so much I can do.

I travel to school in the morning,
my teacher greets me at the door.
I can't wait to go into my classroom.
It's a place I love to explore.

I like it when the children
wave hello to me each day.
I love to make new friends,
who can laugh with me and play.

I like to visit the countryside,
taking walks out on the farm.
I like to feed the animals,
who make me happy and feel calm.

Being with my family,
is my favourite place to be.
They make me smile and make me laugh.
They never stop loving me.

So now you know I have Hydrocephalus
and the things I love to do,
Something I would love to know,
is what abilities are in you?

Write down your super abilities:

_____

_____

_____

_____

What makes you happy?
Please *draw* below.

What is hydrocephalus?

Hydrocephalus is a condition where fluid builds up in the head which can affect how the brain works in different ways.

1 in every 1000 babies born are affected by hydrocephalus.

Hydrocephalus is the most common reason for a child to have a brain operation.

As a result of injury or infection, anyone could be affected by hydrocephalus at any point in their life.

Information provided by Shine
Registered Charity No: 249338

Shine is the UK's leading charity for people affected by hydrocephalus and spina bifida. Offering specialist advice pre-birth and throughout life, it's national support and development service provides a lifeline for members, empowering them to lead the lives they want to live. Members can seek support with issues around health, education, benefits and condition management.

Shine's website provides a comprehensive library of resources, whilst members gain access to peer support through a range of online communities, as well as the chance to share their experiences at training and networking events in their area.
Cuts to statutory funding mean the need for these services has never been greater.

Helpline: 01733 555988

Email: firstcontact@shinecharity.org.uk

Web www.shinecharity.org.uk

/ShineUKCharity

@ShineUKCharity

Spina Bifida Hydrocephalus Scotland (SBH Scotland) provide a lifetime commitment of specialist support and information to all those affected by these hydrocephalus and/or spina bifida including family members, carers and healthcare professionals. Created in 1965 by parents for parents and their children, over 50 years later SBH Scotland keep individuals at the heart of everything they do. SBH Scotland's Support Team work across Scotland with a range of services including: a helpline, one-to-one support in homes and schools, clinics, support groups, financial advice, play sessions and workshops. A range of resources and information can also be found on their websites.

Helpline: 03455 211 300

Email: support@sbhscotland.org.uk

Web: www.sbhscotland.org.uk

Web: www.hydrocephalusscotland.org.uk

/SBHScotland

@SBHScotland

The Hydrocephalus Association is a national non-profit whose mission is to find a cure for hydrocephalus and improve the lives of those impacted by the condition.

To learn more about hydrocephalus, visit the Hydrocephalus Association:

Web: www.hydroassoc.org

/HydroAssoc

@HydroAssoc

About the Author

My name is Gemma Keir, I am the book author for "The abilities in me" children's book series from Hertfordshire, England. I am a mum to a child with a range of medical conditions, including 22q Deletion who has inspired me to write these incredible stories. I am proud to have received qualifications in Special Educational Needs and Disabilities and Sensory Awareness plus specialist training in Behaviour and Safeguarding. These books provide awareness of a range of needs in children today and will be extremely popular for school settings and families who have a child with these conditions. I aim to change the whole perception of these children by promoting the abilities they do have and prevent potential bullying later in that child's life. I feel that this is possible, because children around them will be taught, from a young age and in a positive light, to have awareness and be open-minded. My vision is for children with special educational needs and disabilities to have a book to read about a character who is just like them. I aim to bring inclusivity to children's literature, acceptance and positivity.

www.theabilitiesinme.com

www.facebook.com/theabilitiesinmebookseries

About the Illustrator

My name is Adam Walker-Parker, I am a professional illustrator from Scotland. I have worked in the art industry for 12 years now, I began my career as an artist, choosing to paint figurative and wildlife paintings.
I now illustrate children's books and find joy in creating something magical and inspiring for children to see.

www.awalkerparker.com

www.facebook.com/awalkerparkerillustration

www.instagram.com/awalkerparkerillustration

MORE BOOKS COMING SOON

We create children's picture books, based on characters of young children with varying disabilities. Each book will feature a child with a condition, and we aim to create a bright, colourful and positive outlook on every child with special needs. We are all unique and beautiful in every way, shape and form. This collection of books will show how each child can celebrate their abilities within their disability, find acceptance and create awareness to those around them. These books will touch the hearts of your homes, schools and hospital settings, and most importantly, your child will have a book to read, based on a special character, just like them.

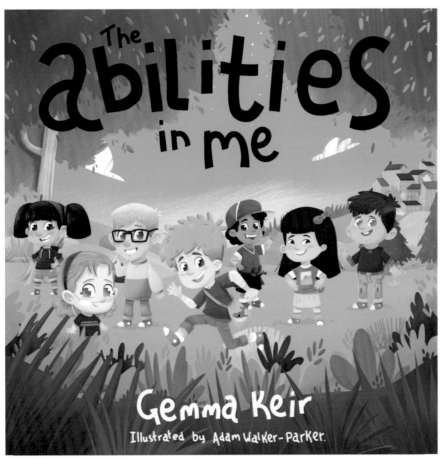

Title: The Abilities In Me - Children's Book Series
Written by Gemma Keir
Cover and Illustrations by Adam Walker-Parker

The abilities in me

BS - #0006 - 060720 - C34 - 216/216/2 [4] - CB - 9781784566982